Winner of the L. E. Phillabaum Poetry Award for 2010

Why the House Is Made of Gingerbread

[poems]

AVA LEAVELL HAYMON

*for Carlos
and yr very special
niche in our
poetry in Louisiana -

Ava*

Louisiana State University Press ✳ Baton Rouge

Published by Louisiana State University Press
Copyright © 2010 by Ava Leavell Haymon
All rights reserved
Manufactured in the United States of America
First printing

Designer: Barbara Neely Bourgoyne
Typefaces: Scala Sans, display; Whitman, text
Printer and binder: Thomson-Shore, Inc.

Library of Congress Cataloging-in-Publication Data
Haymon, Ava Leavell.
  Why the house is made of gingerbread : poems / Ava Leavell Haymon.
    p. cm.
  ISBN 978-0-8071-3585-3 (cloth : alk. paper) — ISBN 978-0-8071-3586-0
(pbk. : alk. paper)
  I. Title.
  PS3608.A945W47 2010
  811'.6—dc22
                                                    2009021202

to my mother, who read me the old stories over and over, as many times as I wanted, from the scuffed up Childcraft with an orange cover, printed toward the end of the war when there was no ink for color pictures

Why not be wholly changed into fire?

ABBOT LOT, fourth century

CONTENTS

EVERYGIRL SINGS HERSELF
AN OLD LULLABY

EVERY STORY MAKES ITS WAY HOME

ACKNOWLEDGMENTS

As this collection of poems underwent transmutation into sequence, some of the individual poems were significantly revised. Titles have changed, titles have moved from one poem text to another, whole poems have been divided and absorbed into others. The author thanks and humbly asks forgiveness from the editors of the following periodicals, in whose pages some of these words previously appeared in some form:

Bellingham Poetry Review: "What Gretel Learned from the Witch," "What the Smoke Knows" (as "Pose, Flammable"); Crab Orchard Review: "The Witch Has Told You a Story"; Louisiana Literature: "Heft" and "How One Became Two"; New Orleans Review: "What Gretel Learned from Her Father" (much revised here and retitled "What Gretel Learns from the Wind"); Nightsun: "Cradlesong"; Northwest Review: "What the Witch Wanted"; Pleiades of the Stars: "Cornbread" (text appearing in several poems in this book), "What Never Happened," (text appearing in several poems, primarily "Autobiography"), "Lunch Break" (as "Invitation"); Prairie Schooner: "Cornucopia"; Rose & Thorn: "Everygirl's Mandala," "The First Wish," "Riddle"; Southern Review: "Why the House Is Made of Gingerbread" (text divided among several poems in this collection)

"Chill Seeping Out of the Old Forest" first appeared as "Woman Alone in the Woods" in the 1991 volume Kitchen Heat (Maude's Head Press). "What the Smoke Knows" was reprinted (as "Pose, Flammable") in Letters to the World: Poems from the Wom-po LISTSERV (Red Hen Press, 2008).

Why the House Is Made of Gingerbread

How One Became Two

When Gretel was small, she told
the secret no one must ever tell.
The ironing board stood between

her and her mother, the woman ironing.
What Gretel remembers is this: the iron
sliding across the backs of her hands

and the freezing cold
that came at first and spread
up her arms to her chest

and how she stood back from the board
awed, the odd meat smell,
the woman's long hair striking

the air like cottonmouths,
the single whir of the clock
and the way it did not proceed.

How Gretel herself seemed to grow
a little taller, sandals and sunsuit gone
and her clothes become a white wool robe

and how her hair went white blond
and floated straight and fine
on air currents the skin could not feel,

mouth falling open slow motion
in nothing more than surprise,
eyes fixed flat as an icon's.

The iron made a clucking sound
and her hands—while she was staring
at them, cold as snow—

ignited. Flamed up yellow-red
like fire forced before bellows—and
it was all she could see,

those burning hands. What might
they do? What could she touch
they would not destroy?

The clock lurched forward at last,
and she fell back and ran to the mirror.
She thought she'd see the child

in white wool with burning hands,
but instead of one she saw two—
twins, a boy and a girl.

The girl, with only a small diminishment
in weight, looked down at her hands,
opening and closing. She could see

every line, knuckle, scar, unmistakable
as initials. The boy felt quite hollow
and set about learning to do

all over again. He found
he was very clever
and always afraid.

That was a different mother.
That was before the story began.

EVERYGIRL HUNGRY

Most cooking, even of elaborate dishes, is merely the combining of a number of very simple operations.

The James Beard Cookbook

Tell me what you eat, and I will tell you what you are.

ANTHELME BRILLAT-SAVARIN

The Candle House

Gretel's kept it in the Christmas decorations
for years, setting it out every holiday season
with crèches, nutcrackers, earnest clay blobs
the children painted in kindergarten.

This year she's decided to light it, strikes
a wooden kitchen match and holds it
to the wick, a twist of string
surfacing through paraffin snow

near the chimney. Several false starts
and it blazes up, crackles with surprise
at discovering its own function, settles in
to burn like any cheerful votive.

The flame steadies. A little puddle scoops
in the roof beam. The candle is a fire
now, confident of its own appointed fuel.
The house is burning itself down.

Gretel keeps it with her, after she's pushed
red bows and strings of lights onto the shelf
of an upstairs closet and the living room's
quieted down, drafty and plain. She lights it

in the kitchen when she loads the dishwasher
and beside her on the counter where she writes
the thank you notes. Worrying how to make
the kids write theirs, she stares at it, half gone,

peaked gables glaring back hollow triangle eyes.
Fire crater halfway down, the windows
reveal themselves parchment under wax—
not a sugar glaze at all—and a guttering light

inside flickers through. Gretel
remembers a dark soot basement, herself
eight years old, the grates in a coal furnace,
red glow nodding through split sheets of mica.

The fire is at the bottom. Shredded walls
spindle around it, a collapsing well.
Where will the fire go now? Which part
the first to fail? It seems dangerous

to leave it alone, not to tend it constantly.
When the candle house is completely gone,
Gretel thinks to herself, the patient little flame
could spread anywhere.

Recipes from a Family *Grimoire*

Ordinary house, kitchen,
ordinary American city.
Gretel, whipping up a family
supper for the customary

husband, children, reaches under
the cabinet for her grandmother's
cast-iron skillet, and begins
remembering her childhood

and it's not at all the way it happened.
It's the story with the girl
whose name was also Gretel, the one
everybody knows about, lost in the woods

with the boy, her brother. She was baking
strawberry tarts when the voice first spoke:
I learned this from the witch.
As today, careful not to lick the spoon,

she is stirring cornbread batter, mixing buttermilk
into cornmeal and eggs without measuring,
the addition not a prescription in fraction and noun
but a habit of her wrists and hands.

She is alone for once, the silent house
brooding her own small cooking
noises. From the oven, set on preheat,
a hot-metal *plink*—

Gretel stops, hands checked
midmotion, a yellow baking soda box
tilted and pouring white powder
into her curled palm. Says aloud:

Who am I
that my life becomes
this story?

Fairy-Tale Childhood

Gretel's childhood unrolls toward the past,
plain and unelaborated as grudging
bedtime stories, a thumbnail biography

with no messy events such as trouble
the afternoon—she's waiting for
the plumbers, nervous she'll miss them

while she drives car pool. She remembers
no trips to the drug store, no gathering up
books to take to school, no waiting—

now she spends so much time waiting.
But surely as a child she spent more, she thinks—
a child waits for dessert, for turns,

for birthdays, rides, summertime,
waits for Daddy to come home
before anyone can eat supper.

The insistent new version of her childhood:
uncluttered clashes among simple forces, a death
struggle. In short, a fairy tale,

one which calls for hero children—girl and boy—
always lively and frequently lucky,
and maybe the standard reward at the end.

She looks back at this childhood
and asks: Who was Hansel?
Why was it I who had to kill the witch?

Why does the story begin with the mother
dead? The walls of gingerbread—
they were not on plumb. They'd yawed

against each other, skidded sideways a bit
till the eggwhites in the icing set hard.
Who raises, who braces walls with only sugar?

Everygirl's Mandala

First, a large gold circle on the page,
drawn freehand. Someone told her to begin
that way, and Gretel is nothing
if not obedient. Inside the circle,

she draws a lopsided cube, brown,
adds a roof on top, triangle and plane:
a little house, a gingerbread house.
And Gretel feels its pull

on a hungry child, the bite of her own desire
for sweets, forbidden sweets. She smudges
white over red for peppermint shingles,
and the house begins to hiss: *No recipe*

will ever satisfy this desire. Its name,
shame, the ultimate disobedience, fat.
Her breathing shallow, Gretel draws stick bodies
with circle heads, wobbling away from her

along gingersnap stepping stones.
The twin children are a surprise,
like pleated paper, scissor-cut,
unfolding all at once into paper dolls.

Above their heads, Gretel scribbles
massed leaves, ponderous tree trunks.
Thick roots lower a great bulk
down past the circle, purple darkens

the sky. The gold circle
is almost gone. Gretel's secret:
sugar melted to dark brown,
butter stirred in, and she, bent over
the kitchen counter lightheaded,

nauseated, mood shuffling from stupid
to cranky, no trace in sink or refrigerator.
Gretel blackens the inside edge of a shadow
and wonders: Where is the witch?

Inside the house looking out? Hiding behind trees,
cackling under her breath that her bait has attracted
its prey? Is she in the sky somehow, sailing back
from who knows where to witness this arrival?

And then Gretel sees her—her two eyes
are the round heads of the lost children,
her jagged nose line cuts through
the hands they hold tight. Below that,

the last curve of gold smirks into a mouth.
Gretel squeezes the red crayon in her fist,
stabs preschooler zigzags for teeth.
She squints and sees all the rest—

black eyebrows bristle troubled auras
above the little heads, coarse hair flails
out past the edge of the page.
Gretel blinks:

Two pictures float without touching.
The first one sketchy, a house
in the woods, red-pink peppermints
smeary on the roof, lost girl and boy.

The second, in hard distinct lines,
a witch's face hanging free,
stark as a wire mobile twisting
on its string. That face, swinging

on its own—is it looking in at the children,
clutching each other and tottering forward
on stiff little legs? Gretel can see it that way,
see through the back of the witch's head

to the scene unfolding in the clearing,
to the children she planned to cook and eat.
But Gretel knows that's false. It's drawn
the way anyone draws a face, even a smiley face

on a dusty table. Those eyes boring crazily
out the backs of the children's coin-round heads,
squiggle of scarlet at the corner
of the awful mouth:

The witch is looking straight out at her.

Autobiography

Gretel's attention disengages from her driving
and she is the young girl in the dark
beside Hansel's cage, legs aching from standing
since before dawn. Gretel squeezes
the wheel, shoulders tight, longing

to trade places with her brother,
for his ignorance of minding the fire,
hauling water with bruised fingers,
his freedom from the danger of failure—one slip
of the girl's memory in a recipe, one broken dish

and there's no story, just another couple of kids
who never came home. A ruckus breaks out
in the back seat, and Gretel shudders back
into the present, driving kids to school.
She presses the brake hard: *That didn't happen!*

I never had a brother, there was no shortage
of food, no stones to mark the way, certainly
no clearing or gingerbread house. I was not
abandoned for a cycle of seasons in thrall
to a witch. I didn't murder a crone

in her own oven. I had real sisters,
no brother at all. I walked to school by myself
and walked back home again. No detail
to that history, no taste or smell.
The unexceptional childhood

Gretel's taken for granted shrinks
to a newspaper article with no photographs,
set in a place she's never seen with her own eyes.
The yelling in the back seat subsides,
and the story with the brother takes up again.

Gretel slumps back into her seat, gives in
to the girl child's desire for a cage to flail
against, the strike of edges, the immediate *thunk*
of flat roof, for angry tears that come
when the body is exhausted, failed,
the clumsy fall, the dirt floor, sleep.

Lunch Break

She orders the same
as always, plain fish, no bread,
vegetable of the day, iced herb tea.
Self-conscious in the gesturing
and chatter of other tables, she studies
a travel poster near her, mountains

in Europe, evergreens thick and dark.
And now a voice—no more urgent
than lunchtime conversation: *Gretel, Gretel.*
You took my name, you must tell me who I am.
Did I kill the witch, Gretel? Can she be dead,
she who baked the walls of her house on cookie pans?

And how could I leave
my father's house, following the boy?
Where are the crumbs that cried,
Do not go back, you can't go back,
and the flushed thicket birds?
How did Hansel and I become one child,

one with no front—the child no parent slaps
since that child presents no face at all.
Tell me how we knew our way home
after the witch, the way so easy then,
the story tired, impatient to be done,
the boy's legs grown long for his trousers.

Did he speed up when we passed the beech tree
right at dark, the matted leaves and moss
where we slept when we came that way before?
You can tell me, Gretel, but I am sunk in your body,
my ears made of your flesh—how will I hear

what you say? The witch split a cake
into layers with a thread, a single hair of my head
divides your viscera and heart. The damp cavities
of your body fill with my disappointments,
the air of the forest, clammy at snowmelt
with wet branches and the bother of flies.

Her plate arrives. Gretel nods automatic
thanks. The voice had spoken before,
but never when she was not by herself.
Gretel can no longer pretend she is alone.
The voice is speaking louder.

—for Renata

SMELL OF BAKING

. . . burn it without fear in a dry fire, . . . when you have the true white, then follows the false and citrine colour; and at last the perfect redness itself. This is the glory and the beauty of the whole world.

ROGER BACON, *The Root of the World*, thirteenth century

The Witch Has Told You a Story

You are food.
You are here for me
to eat. Fatten up,
and I will like you better.

Your brother will be first,
you must wait your turn.
Feed him yourself, you will
learn to do it. You will take him

eggs with yellow sauce, muffins
torn apart and leaking butter, fried meats
late in the morning, and always sweets
in a sticky parade from the kitchen.

His vigilance, an ice pick of hunger
pricking his insides, will melt
in the unctuous cream fillings.
He will forget. He will thank you

for it. His little finger stuck every day
through cracks in the bars
will grow sleek and round,
his hollow face swell

like the moon. He will stop dreaming
about fear in the woods without food.
He will lean toward the maw
of the oven as it opens

every afternoon, sighing
better and better smells.

What Gretel Learns from the Wind

Water had run
under their father's house
when it rained hard—a background
sound that undermined their sleep,

a mumble that couldn't be helped
and had no name. At midnight
in the old forest, by then
certain no one would come

to help, Gretel turned to Hansel
for the consolation they had found
together when this fear bound them
the first time—twins, womb-mates, water

rushing even then. And when the food
was gone and rain already sharp with sleet.
It was different for her this time, Hansel
a child still, while she'd grown older.

She stared up into inky branches, listened
to the cough of snow owls. He'd gone to sleep
on her shoulder, breathing through his mouth.
She heard the old rainwater moving, a current

the wind rode through night trees.
The sound said the story would end,
the danger not kill them. Hansel would grow
into another father. Gretel pursed her lips

like an old woman—he would not remember
any of this. For a moment she knew
everything: Hansel would crack walnuts
against each other in his huge hands,

and she would grow up to hear
the sound of water, again and again,
no matter where she went,
no matter how hard she tried.

The First Wish

Knowing the sugar house
dangerous, even evil, Gretel walked
toward it. After long enough in the woods,

any house of your own kind seems a shelter.
They had seen dens, lair, deer huddles,
small round nests of finches.

An adult might think these sweet,
her eyes go soft when she fumbles
onto little wads of flannel and hay

the brown mouse lays down in the firewood
or a cocoon webbed soft to a stem in the weeds.
But a child, her hands chapped and cold,

a child without a mother has no luxury
of sentiment—finding such things,
she sees only the eggs she might eat

if she's desperate enough by that time,
or the return of another female
to run at her with claws or slapping wings.

The smell of baking paralyzed
Gretel's good sense, fondant
congealing from clear to snow,

a house cooking itself up
before her eyes, because her eyes
fixed on it. Hansel, in his headlong way,

had crashed through the willow break
at the clearing's edge, grabbing for candy
curlicues, yelling out her name.

One step, another, her face slackening
into a baby's. Houses could be warmth,
could be safety, company, soft dry beds.

But this one was food.
The first wish.
Food.

First Bond

Before even a taste
of rock-candy icicle—
the boy's cheeks

stuffed with gingerbread—
Gretel stretched her face
toward a window of the house

hoping for a reflection, her first
since the twins were abandoned.
The sockets of a skull

jumped into focus, broken-twig
hands lifting in astonishment to tap
skin crust, gray cheekbones.

Gretel gasped
at the change:
Thin, thin,

lost, nothing to eat,
I didn't know we were
in the forest so long.

Inside the house, looking
out the unglazed window,
the witch forgets

she'd forgotten mirrors.
She is touching her own face
for the first time in years.

Myself, she says: *a child.*
I'm young. I'm young.

What the Witch Wanted

The witch is willing to live out
the story, follow the recipe
faithful as an acolyte, trust
events to uncurl in their sleepy way,

to let dough rise in the crock
without peeking,
do her meticulous part
and wait for the rest—

the children always come along
ready or not, boy child and girl child,
eyes round as faith, stomachs
hurting for food, for love—

this time, it is perfect.
Scrappy boy gets them through
the woods, the girl clever, strong,
quick hand at the batter, a knack

for proportions and spices.
Relief to the tired witch heart
that's waited for this adept:
The knowledge will not be lost.

So many failed years
when the children arrived
but were not hungry enough,
or they died of fear in the forest

or the girl would not learn
the formulas, or they stayed
without struggle to be cooked
and eaten. Easy enough

to kill those, but centuries pass
to cycle events around this way
again. This time, the story
satisfies like a dumpling.

The girl is sensible, the boy will not
get in the way. The lore will
be passed on, the season turn
in a quiet blessing of pedagogy.

This time—she laughs outright—
this time, the witch can die.

What Gretel Learns from the Witch

To break eggs with decision,
to shave the nutmeg fine enough,
to wait for butter to soften on its own.
Kitchen habits: a fixed rhythm
of hunger and nourishment,

a compact between eater and eaten,
old as mouths—the message encoded
in every recipe, passed down
for generations right under
the polished history of those in charge.

Control the heat, the witch grumped—
she disliked speaking
in generalities—*in the way you feed
the fire.* Gretel absorbed
the first instructions in desperation

to keep herself and her brother alive.
And then—because the knowledge changed
her—she could learn anything
the witch had to teach, memorized
as though she'd known all along.

More wood, stupid girl—
the witch hated to repeat her orders.
Inside the thick walls of the oven,
the fire ruffled softly and sent out
a crackle of sparks.

Everygirl Practices Deceit

They would squeeze the bars, choose
the thinnest—the witch away at night,
they never knew where. The girl saw
from the outside: birch shoots
thin as babies' wrists, lashed

with strips of cedar bark,
the boy could snap any of them.
Tomorrow night, he'd vow:
I break that one and I'm free.
By morning, he'd put it off again.

Take this, she whispered, giving him
an oak twig rubbed smooth.
This was her first command.
When she asks to feel your finger,
poke the stick through the bars.

The boy was in her power now,
she could tell. He would do whatever
she required. It was the cakes
she could bake almost as well
as the witch. She knew on her tongue

how the cake would taste
after the oven—when it was still batter,
when the brown creamy sludge
needed one smidgen of cardamom, a pinch
of ground cloves. She rolled salt

between finger and thumb, grain by grain.
Her teeth clicked, determined.
She would learn more from the witch.
She would learn everything.

The Blood Time

Blood appeared between
her legs, and Gretel did not know

what it was. She showed it to Hansel,
who whimpered and cowered back

in the corner of the stick cage. The witch
found the cinnamon-colored traces,

came to Gretel in silence, bumped
the young cheek with a veiny hand.

She brought white cloths, a clay bowl
of warmed water, a small copper bracelet

for Gretel's left arm, with a milky green stone,
rough cut. The smell of the circle on her skin

set Gretel's teeth humming, left
a metallic twang on the end of her tongue.

Wear this and count with the moon.
That was what the witch told her.

Everyboy's Accusation

Something hazy nagged at Hansel
about the way Gretel got to be
the focus of the story.
Something from back when

they first arrived at the candy house,
even before their first hunger abated,
while they still believed the old woman
might keep them safe.

Maybe it was when the witch said:
One of you will sleep here. And the twins,
brown taffy clamping their teeth, followed
to see the little sapling box—a house

more primitive than the one made of cakes,
as though the witch's pattern was older
than ovens. He investigated neatly
constructed joins, only half listening,

but didn't Gretel immediately say
how much work she could do in the kitchen?
And didn't there follow a bit of discussion
about how to get a strong little boy to crawl

inside such a trap? Here Hansel's recollection
became quite distinct: Gretel's voice
saying to the witch, *I'll help you.*

Fairy-Tale Pedagogy

She assembled éclairs, puffed pastry
rolled flat over the cold stone and baked hot,
the chocolate filling warm and silky.
The boy would set his mouth

for honey cakes, and he'd snap:
Not what I wanted. Next afternoon
when she brought him honey cake,
he'd pout for éclairs. At last he gave up

wanting one thing and feeling
sorry for himself if he didn't get it
and settled in to despise anything
she brought. When he heard footsteps

cross the sill of the kitchen door, numbness
would seize his face. The two of them
ganged up, he was convinced, so the real events
evolved into narrative without him.

Desperate to please, the girl pushed further,
cooking, as the witch insisted, from smell, not taste—
herbs from the kitchen garden, roots that grew
a day's walk away, nuts and seeds

only the witch knew how to find.
The old woman watched. Never had a student
come to her who worked so hard to learn. Finally,
there were breads complex from triple rising,

eggwhites beaten to peaks
and black walnuts chopped to fold in.
Hansel turned his face to the side,
went days without meeting Gretel's eyes.

The witch clucked to herself,
satisfied. Gretel would try
even harder.

Year's Turn

A late summer sunbeam slanted inside
and reddened to amber. Gretel reached
the broom into corners, teasing
the dot of color. The girl's

limber movements set the witch
muttering: *Fields of grain with no shade,*
knife that keeps its edge. A few words—
Bees and candles, year's turn—

growled into Gretel's hearing,
fumbled words that twisted
the stiff mouth. Gretel saw sooty teeth.
She took a breath to ask something,

but the plaything of light
withdrew, and the dirty floor
had to be swept clean
before it was too dark to see.

Everygirl Dreams of Apples

Peeling apples, too many apples
to remember to be afraid,
Gretel's steady hands slowed.

Dawdling! snapped the witch
and pinched the waiting crust.
Lumps! Use the mesh, stupid girl.

And that night, Gretel dreamed
a mother in another kitchen, ironing,
the room sweet with hot cotton,

waxed paper, shirts from the line,
and behind that, like a promise,
. apples baking, apples baking.

The smell pulled a dream girl
toward a dream mother. Next morning,
Gretel's spice cakes rose

to their full size, and puddinglike
spots at the centers sprang
back after a tender touch.

Gretel doubled hot pads
on the edges of cake pans
and lifted them out to cool.

Oven heat poured out against old burns.
She wanted the dream again
but it was gone.

The Riddle

Trying once again to produce
a butter cream—cool room, cool
crockery, wooden spatula, wooden spoon—

the girl forgot the witch and imagined
the taste in the boy's mouth.
Under her hands she felt the sugar
relinquish its crystal grit

without dissolving, and the butter,
without melting, relax its waxy
resistance. Butter and sugar
disappeared, and there it was

at last—the smooth paste, neither solid
nor liquid, somewhere in between.
Keep your fingers out! And a hard slap,
like the stepmother's.

Gretel's flaring cheek asked a new question:
What if I try hard enough? Learn everything?
Without taking a single taste, produce the cake
that makes the boy smile and grow fat?

Then she roasts Hansel in the fire
and dances all night in her dark garden.
I'll be the only child here and no use to her
alive. The spoon was lifting

butter cream, perfect and undeniable.
Gretel's grip loosened, and the spoon swung
sideways like the needle of a compass.
There is something more, she thought:

something the witch will never teach me.
A riddle of kitchens, so plain
I can't see it, the answer physical
as gristle in the riddle itself.

Her wrist dropped,
spoon plopped into bowl.
Perfect apprentice, heroine girl,
the complete cook must learn to kill.

How a Good Girl Learns to Kill

The little birds, rabbits
caught in her simple snares,

these were easy once
the knife was sharp.

But to kill the witch,
Gretel had to give up

the first mother.
With the usual prayers

and talismans, she tried
to summon her, but the arms,

the milky smell receded,
mirror under deepening water.

She sang the old songs,
the hard lullabies, stared down

the amber-flecked eyes of scavenger
birds, chanted herself back

into the basket of feathers, finally
into the great red cave,

water-flooded, where the twins
swam, supple as otters.

There, great fish crowded
in, toothed mouths,

eels kinked in seaweed
and the water cooling,

cooling, then cold.
They were not separate then,

not boy and girl, but when
Hansel turned his face away,

Gretel knew at last
she was alone.

EVERYGIRL SINGS HERSELF
AN OLD LULLABY

––––––––

It is said that during the Black Death in Europe, orphaned
babies were sometimes swaddled in cloth slings hung in trees
and abandoned to die. This practice may have given rise to
the familiar nursery song.

Cradlesong

I

Rock-a-bye baby   *in the treetop*
when the wind blows   *the cradle will rock*
when the bough breaks   *the cradle will fall*
and down will come baby   *cradle and all*

Rock-a-bye baby   *in the tree top*
when the wind blows   puff of hot air
the cradle will rock   cloth sling moving,
                          womb-carried
when the bough breaks   swing high
              fall back the other way

Rock-a-bye baby   too high
                          too high
in the tree top   where?   who?   am I?
              will come for me?   left me here?

Rock-a-bye baby   *in the treetop*
                          too high, too bumpy
when the wind blows   whose   baby   am   I?

the cradle   Whose baby am I now?

II

Fire scream   Mother rises out of solid rock
Iron teeth scrape sharp   on feldspar, on escape
tempering   as she smelts her way free

Glowing metal   against my cool skin
She is at me now   my flat breasts
my throat, my wrists   round stomach
soft   an unprotected spring field

III

Beyond the pain and tearing
is the wrongness of it

it is her breasts I should eat
her nipples I should pull at
her soft thighs I should glut myself on

beyond the pain is the wrongness of it

IV

Updraft howls   out of the cave
too frightened   bronze ribs
without breasts   mother without face

too small   I pushed her
the cave   the rocks   too small
everything I had in my hands
too small   too frightened

V

It was to save myself   I pushed her
to save myself   when she turned
her breast to chalk   her breasts

my useful delight   my land of all trees
of crickets singing   fuzzy moths
wild honey   first pillow

against my sleepy face   blasted, blasted
breast to sulfur   crushed
sweet nipple   to chips of flint

to save myself   I had to save myself
to save myself   I pushed her

VI

Baby-rage without means
baby-rage without weapons
clenched fists   arched back
dominion promised   denied

her eyes flick   she looks away
piles of rocks   propped lintels
shaky foundations   I lunge

the stones are upon her   she is underneath
with shale and the seams of coal
I kick with the strength of all babies
all the babies she would eat

she flicked her eyes away
they froze to mica   my nipple to flint

when she turned her eyes
when she blasted my pillow

to save myself   I moved against her

VII

After that, there were years of peace
On the hillside, berries, wild apricots
I sucked my fingers to go to sleep
hummed the old lullabies when I felt afraid

Years of peace, an altar, a forked antler
with the holy curve of her groin
violets, doves' feathers, twig of red maple
a flat stone scratched with the shape
of her breasts   sucked my fingers
to go to sleep   sleep   in my sleep
         I call her name

VIII

I call her name   and she rises, rises
from the smoke slit at my hallowed place
at first slowly   where I am sleeping

sleeping   where I've brought her
colored stones for the changing of the moon
I call her name in my sleep   I am dreaming

she comes from the earth   like a dream
she comes from my body   like a dream
her hair first   floating wild in a red heat

I say her name   a poison butterfly
patient   wet   mechanical
pushes from the chrysalis of my throat

IX

There   my graven tablets
I   among stones, my stones
wake   to the strike of anvils

and she is out   mask cast
in a smithy of root tendrils
jaw a bronze hinge   squalling

hammered talons   chariot craft
gained   when I buried her alive
broken glass   blown glass new to the earth

she is at me again   this flesh hers again
my fat   runs off her chin
long as I resist   I am the feast

long as I resist   the feast is endless

this new dispensation   screech of axle
and hub plays the old songs, the cradle songs
and with my final strength

I reach toward her
stretch up both arms
in my great desire to hear

X

Rock-a-bye baby   in the treetop
when the wind blows   the cradle will rock
when the bough breaks   the cradle will fall
and down

                and down and down

when the bough breaks   the cradle will fall
and down

          and down
and down
      to the mother
         who put me here

down will come

          stay up   stay up
    whose baby am I?

when the
      wind blows me
          back down to her

wind
      wish wind—magic baby—

blows
      me to her   mother
        who wants me here

the cradle

         above her eyes

down will come

         up here, up here

baby   cradle   and all

EVERY STORY MAKES ITS WAY HOME

———————

No one has lifted my veil.

Inanna's Song

Here Is a Girl

Gray and black with carbon
from too many fires, here is the stove,
heating slowly to a dull orange.

Bright lines outline the thick door
with a flashing white-yellow that defeats
daylight from the deep window.

Here is the fire chamber, noisy
with juniper knots, the *shush-shush*
of slow-burning ash wood.

And here is a girl drawn with charcoal,
lines too thin to bear a woman's weight,
her destiny upon her now, the plot

prescribing murder. Even a stick figure
implies a heart. How could she kill
this old woman, the last woman

the story gives her? The witch
issues a final instruction:
Crawl inside, check the heat.

The empty circle head bobs. Danger,
under the words' surface. *Show me,*
says the stick girl: *I don't know how.*

Narrative stalls. The two
face each other, about the same size.
Here is another sound—*flump*—

logs and flaming branches rearrange
themselves in the cast-iron chamber.
The woman turns,

hooks an arthritic knee
over the stone ledge. The stick girl
fills with flesh definite as poured milk.

Strong shoulder, new weight,
she heaves the witch up and in
and closes the door.

What the Smoke Knows

It is over. The fire,
when it comes at last, a relief.
The pose had been flammable as gauze,
a black rag skirt, the shawl
and broom. Her skin, like parchment
anyway, browns first in spots
then flashes into light and heat.

Ridiculous, she thinks to herself
as her eyes all at once give up
their fierce attention, melt
the way water balloons burst in heat,
first the surface tension, then a rush
of steamy center—the pose a fraud
from the beginning. It bought me

time—time and children, this house,
the many meals, the craft. I let them
look at me however they chose—
priests, babies, old men gray as ash.
Each came away with a different story.
Only the children, chastened and generous,
have let me go.

What Gretel Takes with Her

After she slams the oven closed
behind the witch, after she knows
what she's done, after the witch
does not magically burst back
through the door after all,

Gretel runs outside. The door
to the cage has leaned open
on its own, and he is slumped
in the corner, plump and formless
as undercooked bread pudding.

Come out! There's meanness
in the voice. Where is her wiry brother,
protection in every anxious sinew?
Her cheeks puff out with disgust.
Cakes, bread, he whines:

Don't eat me. She catches sight of
her own arms, scrawny shoulders
where little sharp pains keep her awake
now at night. With Hansel in the cage
they have changed places somehow.

She looks down, sees skinny ribs, small breasts
sore against them. Hears her voice lower,
slowing: *Do what I say.* Sees she is
the last woman in the story, as her mother
was the first, many adventures ago.

Shoves Hansel in the direction of home
and father, takes nothing in her hands,
no stones, no crumbs, shoves him toward
the ending, where there is no happiness
ever after, not in any version.

Heft

What will she do, outside the forest,
knowing the push she gave
the witch? The smell of scorched sugar
on her hands won't rinse off,

the buzz along her hairline
after testing the ginger.
Over and over, she asks herself:
How else could the story go?

Something more,
her muscles keep trying to say:
another side to this, a darker path.
Not enough heft, insists her shoulder:

a little too easy to topple the witch
into the fire and clang home
the cast-iron door. Always
she concludes: No choice.

It had to be played out this way,
the stick through the bars of the cage,
crumbs shining on the path, even
the drip of white glaze off the eaves.

What did the old woman want
in there, something she couldn't have
any other way? Gretel sees the hair
frizzle up, each hair rising,

tips glowing red like dogs' eyes
in the dark. Hears, is still hearing,
the sound of the witch
beginning to laugh.

Everyboy Returns

How did they find their way back,
through the wild places

that baffled them so before,
to the house where it all began?

Is Hansel's the part of the story
not told this time—this stretch of time

the old text races through in a single sentence?
Does Hansel, speechless one, learn words,

when they pass the tree where they slept
on moss and evergreen needles,

where they huddled together, care
and betrayal, night and afternoon, all distinctions

lost in fear and hunger? For the tale
to wind on to the end, they must get home,

reunite with the failed father—poor Hansel,
wobbly kneed still, is this his task?

They walk into blind sunlight at last,
and Hansel looks back over his shoulder

at footprints scuffing along
behind them in the dust of the path.

Wonders why he couldn't see
footprints the first time, smaller

footprints that must have followed them
when they walked the other way so long ago.

Chill Seeping Out of the Old Forest

You have eaten the gingerbread house,
my children. Left me
in changing weather. Every evening,

the sun goes down earlier.
I was so anxious to fatten you up,
I failed to save crumbs
to mark my way home.

The Spell Lifts

Puff of gray smoke, whiff
of evergreen sap, and the terror
is gone. Cookie house collapses

into a story for children, a household tale.
To add a picture, the cage, chimney,
ring of tall trees release their color

and lie down flat on the page.
Common childhood surfaces:
sisters, school, unremarkable

neighborhood, father, mother.
Seven years, Gretel's memory
kidnapped by her namesake,

and now, without ceremony, here
is her own house again. Her husband
asks no questions. The children

have grown up, moved away,
one, then the other. Every birthday,
she has shipped a homemade cake

to summer camps, dorm rooms,
apartments, tucked in
palm-sized packages of candles.

Hansel, his sister who saved him,
the stepmother, the father, they lose all
characteristics, they fail like wax

figurines melted down for reuse.
In afternoon light, in the ordinary kitchen,
Gretel sees what no one else can:
old burns across the backs of her hand.

Cornucopia

The witch, what of her?
She would wait, neither happy
nor unhappy. She had cooked
herself up after all

and could do so again, exist
as undeniably in recipe form
as in a cake slice on the saucer.
A rite of passage cake—

we've forgotten the name—
the cake a girl bakes
when she lets go of her mother
and founds her own kitchen.

It lies in our memory, irreducible
as grandmothers, packed away
in attic trunks with moldering
crazy quilts, string-creased packets

of letters in formal illegible script.
Sometimes it's in the body, little pains
in the shoulder, the strained neck
we should not have at our age.

The witch came to Gretel finally
in a dream, clenching her cobwebby bundle
in a death clutch. Then a gesture
so small there was no plot, no drama at all.

Gretel almost missed it.
The scraggy hands softened.
That was all that happened.
Softened and opened the way

your hands do when you reach
toward the face of a sick three-year-old.
You mean to test for fever,

but your hands say:
The good in the body is deep.
And next day the child is chasing
her playmates beneath a flashing sun.

The witch's hands warmed, sagged open
a fraction, released her dusty offering.
Smell of cedar, mold, anise, candle wax.
Snips of paper and dry leaves

fluttered out both ends, but most of it—
the dream insisted—the wildcraft gist,
the cornucopia, remained.
Gretel woke, her own hands warm,

the palms and fingers now
as warm as the burn scars.
It was the oven fire again,
no longer so harsh. That was all.